HISTORY & GEOGRAPHY 809

AMERICA INTO THE NEW MILLENNIUM

Author:
Theresa Buskey, J.D.
Rachelle Wiersma, M.A., B.A.

Editor:
Alan Christopherson, M.S.

Media Credits:
Page 3: © Fuse, iStock, Thinkstock; **5:** Ollie Atkins, N.A.R.A; **7:** © Fuse, Thinkstock; Byron E. Schumaker, N.A.R.A.; **8:** Robert Knudsen, N.A.R.A.; **10:** N.A.R.A.; **11:** David Hume Kennerly; **12:** © Library of Congress; **14:** David Falconer, N.A.R.A.; © yelet, iStock, Thinkstock; **15:** Enghelab Eslami Newspaper; **19:** © william87, iStock, Thinkstock; **20:** White House Photographic Office; © Svetl Tebenkova, iStock, Thinkstock; **21:** © Oleg Zabielin, iStock, Thinkstock; **22:** © 1971yes, iStock, Thinkstock; **24:** © Hemera Technologies, AbleStock.com, Thinkstock; **25:** Yuryi Abramochkin, RIA Novosti; **28:** © photoknot, iStock, Thinkstock; © LSP1982, iStock, Thinkstock; **37:** Susan Biddle, N.A.R.A.; © Magcom, iStock, Thinkstock; **38:** © mipan, iStock, Thinkstock; CT Snow; **41:** Bob McNeely, United States Armed Forces; **43:** Eric Draper; Gil Cohen, United States Air Force; National Park Service; **44:** © Jean Nordmann, iStock, Thinkstock; **45:** © David Szabo, iStock, Thinkstock.

All maps in this book © Map Resources, unless otherwise stated.

Alpha Omega
PUBLICATIONS

804 N. 2nd Ave. E.
Rock Rapids, IA 51246-1759

AMERICA INTO THE NEW MILLENNIUM

The end of the second millennium brought many changes to America and its place in the world. America faced many crises and scandals during these years. The Cold War continued after 1970 but the way the United States (U.S.) dealt with it changed. Because of the Vietnam War, the U.S. was less willing to fight communism. As a result the U.S. and the Union of Soviet Socialist Republics (U.S.S.R. or Soviet Union) began to cautiously work together. The U.S. accepted Communist China as the government of that land and tried to work with them. However, the Cold War did not end until communism itself ended in Europe in the 1980s. America was left as the only super power at the close of the second millennium. At the beginning of the new century, full-scale terrorism came to U.S. soil on September 11, 2001. As a result, the U.S. entered Afghanistan and Iraq in an effort to root out those who assisted terrorists. The U.S. also took an active role in helping people around the world during times of natural and man-made disasters.

Objectives

Read these objectives. The objectives tell you what you will be able to do when you have successfully completed this LIFEPAC®. Each section will list according to the numbers below what objectives will be met in that section. When you have finished this LIFEPAC, you should be able to:

1. Identify the presidents of this time and their actions.
2. Describe Détente and the Watergate Scandal.
3. Describe how the Cold War ended and the changes that came.
4. Describe the first Persian Gulf War and the events surrounding it.
5. Describe events in America shortly before and after the New Millennium.

1. FALL OF A PRESIDENT

Richard Nixon could have gone down in history as one of our greatest presidents. He took America out of Vietnam. Then, he began to work with the communists. He hoped to end the Cold War. He was not able to do that, but he did start a time of better relations between the super powers. He also opened talks with Communist China and accepted them as the government of that land. It was a great accomplishment.

However, Richard Nixon was involved in a huge scandal. It was a complicated mess named "Watergate." Because of it, Richard Nixon became the only president in our history to resign from office. He did it to avoid being impeached.

Distrust of the government had grown during the Vietnam War. Watergate made it much worse. The new president, Gerald Ford, quickly became unpopular and was voted out of office in 1976. The next president's lack of experience made him unpopular. He lost the next election in 1980.

Objectives

Review these objectives. When you have completed this section, you should be able to:

1. Identify the presidents of this time and their actions.
2. Describe Détente and the Watergate Scandal.
5. Describe events in America near the turn of the millennium.

Vocabulary

Study these new words. Learning the meanings of these words is a good study habit and will improve your understanding of this LIFEPAC.

evidence (ev' ə dnəs). Facts; proof; anything that shows or makes clear.

innocent (in' ə sənt). Doing no wrong or evil; free from sin or wrong; not guilty.

investigate (in ves' tə gāt). To search into; examine closely.

Islam (is' ləm). The religion based on the teachings of the man Muhammad as they appear in the Koran.

pardon (pärd' n). Forgiveness; to set free from punishment.

productive (prə duk' tiv). Producing, supplying, or bringing about much.

shortage (shôr' tij). Lack; too small of an amount.

technology (tek nol' ə jē). The use of scientific knowledge to solve practical problems; the practical methods used to solve those problems.

tension (ten' shən). A strain; severe or wearing pressure.

Note: *All vocabulary words in this LIFEPAC appear in* **boldface** *print the first time they are used. If you are unsure of the meaning when you are reading, study the definitions given.*

Pronunciation Key: hat, āge, cãre, fär; let, ēqual, tėrm; it, īce; hot, ōpen, ôrder; oil; out; cup, pút, rüle; child; long; thin; /ŦH/ for then; /zh/ for measure; /u/ or /ə/ represents /a/ in about, /e/ in taken, /i/ in pencil, /o/ in lemon, and /u/ in circus.

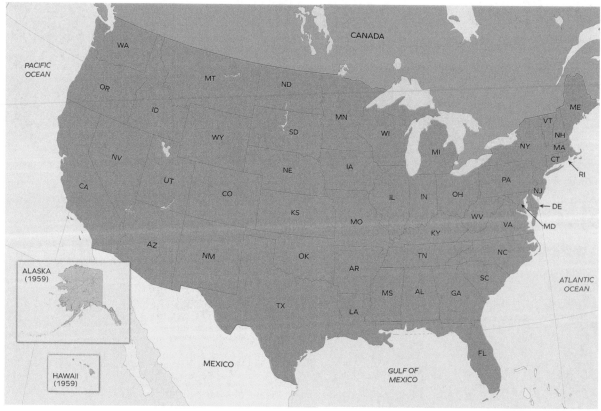

| The United States

Détente

China. President Nixon was well known for how much he disliked communism. However, he realized America did not have the money, men, and willingness to fight communism everywhere. The Vietnam War showed how difficult it could be to fight like that. Therefore, Nixon and his Secretary of State, Henry Kissinger, decided to work with the communists as much as they possibly could.

| Ping-pong was a non-political way for the U.S. and China to interact.

Nixon started with China. Since China had become communist, almost no one from the United States had even visited there. Americans knew very little about the country. However, Nixon realized that China and the U.S.S.R. did not trust each other. He knew that the Soviet Union would not like to see America and China become friendly. He hoped the Soviets would also become friendly to keep China and the U.S. from working together against them. It worked.

China was willing to talk to the United States. Mao Zedong, the extreme communist leader of China, was getting old. Many people within his government wanted trade and business with the West. Some of the first Americans to visit China since the communist takeover were ping-pong players. Ping-pong was very popular in China, so an American team was sent. It allowed the two nations to contact each other in a non-political way.

In 1971 the U.S. allowed Communist China to take the Chinese seat in the United Nations. Taiwan was removed from the United Nations completely. The next year, President Nixon shocked the nation by going to China himself! Henry Kissinger had secretly made the arrangements with the Chinese government. The visit was a huge success.

China had been completely closed to the West since 1949. News reports did not cover what happened there because no one knew much. Even such big events as famines or floods in China might not be known in America. The Chinese government did not tell

| President Richard Nixon was the first U.S. president to 'open up' China (Nixon on the Great Wall).

anyone about them and American reporters were not allowed in the country. Many Americans were very curious about this ancient land. They were anxious to see what would happen when President Nixon visited there.

U.S. television covered everything about the president's visit. The president met with the Chinese leaders, including Mao. He toured some of the famous places in the country built by the old emperors. It was the first time Beijing and the wonders of ancient China had been seen on television. The success of the visit encouraged both sides. They sent representatives to each other's countries to talk more. In 1979 the U.S. accepted the communist government as the *real* government of China.

U.S.S.R. As Nixon had hoped, the Soviet Union was alarmed by the growing friendship between China and America. The new Soviet leader, Leonid Brezhnev, decided to make things better between the U.S. and U.S.S.R. Communism in the Soviet Union also was in trouble. The communist system could not create new **technology** as fast as the Free World. Americans were building newer, faster computers, telephones, and other things. The Soviets needed to trade with the West to get them, because they could not invent them that fast. Brezhnev agreed to let Nixon visit the Soviet Union in 1972.

Richard Nixon was the first American president to visit the Soviet Union. He and Brezhnev signed several important agreements. The most important was SALT, the Strategic Arms Limitation Treaty. It was the first attempt by the super powers to control the atomic arms race. It did not stop the arms race, but it did slow it some.

The new cooperation between the super powers was called *Détente*. The word means a relaxing of anger and **tension** between two people or nations. Détente would last until 1979. It was one of the longest and most **productive** thaws in the Cold War.

Many people hoped Détente would be a way to end the Cold War peacefully, but that did not happen. The Soviet Union was still communist. It was still trying to spread communism by "wars of liberation." It still forced eastern Europe to stay communist. As long as communism existed in the Soviet Union, real peace was impossible.

Many other people thought Détente was a bad idea. They did not trust the Soviet Union and China. They did not believe that they would keep their word if they did agree to things like fewer atomic bombs. They were afraid that the communists would get the Free World to make peace and then attack when we were not ready.

| President Nixon was the first U.S. president to visit the U.S.S.R. (pictured: Nixon and Leonid Brezhnev)

Some of what these people feared was true. Communist governments would never be fully at peace with the Free World. They were too caught up in their own lie that they had a better kind of government that had to take over the world. However, American presidents never gave up on Containment. They kept giving some help to people fighting communism in their countries. The U.S. also never allowed its military to get so weak that the Soviet Union could attack easily. Thus, Détente did not end the Cold War, but it also did not hurt the United States. The Cold War continued, it was just a quieter war.

Complete these sentences.

1.1   Richard Nixon was the first president to visit the communist countries of

_____ and _____ .

1.2   Richard Nixon's Secretary of State was _____ .

1.3   Communist China took the Chinese seat at the United Nations in _____ .

1.4   The leader of the Soviet Union in 1972 was _____ .

1.5   The thaw in the Cold War in the 1970s was called _____ .

1.6   The Soviet Union needed to trade because it could not make new

_____ as fast as the West.

1.7   SALT stands for _____ .

1.8   Even during Détente, the U.S. did not give up on the Cold War policy of

_____ .

1.9   The U.S. recognized the communist government of China in _____ .

1.10 President Nixon's visit to China was completely covered by _____ .

1.11 Nixon and Kissinger decided to work with the _____

as much as possible.

Watergate

Burglary. There was a presidential election in 1972. Democrat George McGovern was running against Republican Richard Nixon, who was trying for a second term. The Democratic Party had its headquarters in the Watergate Hotel in Washington, D.C. On June 17, 1972, five men were arrested when they broke into the Democratic offices there. They were carrying electronic "bugs," devices that would allow them to listen to conversations and telephone calls made by the Democrats. It turned out the men had been hired by the Committee to Re-elect the President, Nixon's people.

Cover-up. President Nixon said that he and his closest advisors did not know about the burglary and had not asked for it. He blamed some of his workers for acting on their own. However, later **evidence** would show that several of Nixon's most important aides knew about the burglary and tried to hide how they were involved. They even lied to the courts about what they knew. President Nixon knew about this and told them to "cover-up" (hide and lie about) what they had done. The whole scandal was named "Watergate."

| Taped conversations between Nixon and his aides proved he was involved in the Watergate Scandal. Nixon resigned to avoid being impeached by Congress.

Investigation. Nixon won the election in November of 1972, but many people did not believe he was completely **innocent** in the Watergate burglary. *The Washington Post*, a newspaper, **investigated** and accused the White House of a cover-up. Early in 1973, a committee in the Senate began to hold hearings to investigate for themselves.

One of Nixon's aides, John Dean, accused him of a cover-up, but there was no proof. Then, in July, the committee learned that President Nixon made tape recordings in his office. All of the talks he had with his aides and helpers were recorded. If the committee could get the tapes of the conversations with John Dean, they would know exactly what the president had been told and what he told his men to do about it!

The committee and the lawyer who was in charge of the investigation, Archibald Cox, asked for the tapes. Nixon refused. The committee and Cox went to court to get them. They won in October. However, Nixon still would not co-operate. He fired Cox and sent some of the tapes, but not the ones that would reveal the truth. The investigation and the controversy continued, as did the arguing in the court case to force Nixon to give up the tapes.

By 1974 enough proof had been collected to arrest several of Nixon's aides. The House of Representatives was considering impeaching the president. Finally, the Supreme Court ruled in July that President Nixon had to give the committee the tapes that he had kept. They were made public on August 5, 1974. They clearly showed that the president had told his men to cover up what they knew about the burglary. That made it certain that he would be impeached by the House. On August 9, 1974, Richard Nixon resigned as president of the United States.

Constitutional success. The long investigation of the president had revealed many things besides just Watergate. In 1973 Vice President Spiro Agnew had resigned from his office because of things that he had done wrong in reporting his taxes. Under the 25th Amendment to the Constitution, the president was allowed to choose a new vice president if one resigned or died. President Nixon chose a replacement for Agnew and the Congress approved his choice. In December of 1973, Congressman Gerald Ford was appointed as the new vice president.

When Nixon resigned in 1974, Ford became president. He was the only man ever to become president who was not elected either president or vice president. He was an appointed president, not an elected one.

The American people were very upset by Watergate, especially when it came so close behind the Vietnam War and the wild protests. People really distrusted the government and their leaders. However, many people pointed out that the Constitution had worked well through the whole scandal. The Congress and courts had been able to use their power to force the president to tell the truth. He had resigned and the Constitution had provided a way to give the nation a new president. America could thank the wonderful planning of the men who wrote the Constitution back in 1787 that all had gone so well.

Reaction. President Ford had a difficult job. No one had voted for him to be president. He was appointed to the vice presidency and moved up only because his president resigned. He made matters worse by giving Richard Nixon a full **pardon**. That meant Nixon could never go to jail for what he had

| President Gerald Ford granted Richard Nixon a full pardon for the Watergate Scandal.

done, which made the nation even more furious. The pardon insured that President Ford would never be a popular president. He basically just filled the office until the next election in 1976.

By 1976 everyone was very sick of the government thanks to Vietnam, Watergate, and the pardon. Ford was the Republican candidate in 1976, but he really had very little chance of winning. The Democratic candidate was the governor of Georgia, James Earl "Jimmy" Carter, Jr. Carter ran as someone who had no part in Watergate or the political games in the capital. He emphasized that he was free of all the Washington mess. He promised a more honest government and won the election. His lack of experience in the federal government got him elected, but it would soon get him in trouble, too.

| President Jimmy Carter

Name the item, event, person, or thing.

1.12 _____ Scandal that forced Richard Nixon to resign

1.13 _____ Lawyer who was in charge of the investigation

1.14 _____ Vice president who resigned in 1973

1.15 _____ The first appointed president in American history

1.16 _____ Newspaper that investigated the scandal

1.17 _____ Date that President Nixon resigned

1.18 _____ Organization that hired the burglars

1.19 _____ Aide that accused Nixon of a cover-up

1.20 _____ Man who was elected president in 1976

Answer these questions.

1.21   What did President Ford do that made the nation angry at him?

_____

1.22   What were the burglars carrying when they broke into the Watergate building?

_____

1.23   Why was Carter elected in 1976?

_____

_____

1.24   What finally proved that Nixon wanted a cover-up?

_____

_____

America in the 1970s

Inflation. One of the biggest problems of the 1970s was something called *inflation*. Inflation is a time when prices go up. During the 1970s prices were going up quickly, more quickly than people's salaries. Prices more than doubled from 1970 to 1980. The quickly rising prices made it hard for people to pay their bills and afford all the things they used to be able to afford. To make matters worse, there were not enough jobs for everyone. The American people expected the government to fix these problems.

President Nixon tried several things to stop inflation. He started by trying to cut government spending. He hoped with the government buying less that prices would not go up as fast. When that and other things did not work, he tried price controls. Price controls make it illegal to raise prices. That did not work either because it was too difficult to enforce the law. For example, if someone made a smaller candy bar and sold it for the same price, was that a price increase or not?

President Ford organized a big effort to end inflation. He called it "Whip Inflation Now" or WIN. It also failed. Inflation was finally slowed by the Federal Reserve Board that controls the national bank system. The "Fed" raised interest rates so high that it was difficult to borrow money. That slowed spending, which slowed buying, which slowed price increases beginning in 1979.

Energy crisis. The *energy crisis* was another big problem of the 1970s. The energy crisis was about a **shortage** of oil for gasoline. It made the cost of gas for cars go up very quickly. The nations that produced oil had organized to form OPEC (the Organization of Petroleum Exporting Countries). OPEC began forcing prices up in the 1970s.

Many of the OPEC nations were Arab countries in the Middle East that were enemies of Israel, a nation supported by the United States. In 1973 some of these nations attacked Israel. Many of the OPEC nations embargoed (refused to export) oil to the United States because it was helping Israel. The embargo lasted for five months. It drove prices up, and many people had trouble even finding fuel for their cars. They often had to wait in long lines for gasoline.

The energy crisis eventually was resolved. The high price of oil encouraged American oil companies to drill more oil wells on home soil. That increased the production of oil, ended the oil shortage, and brought the prices back down. However, eventually America will need to find a new fuel for their cars because the oil in the ground will not last forever.

Camp David Accords. Israel had been at war with her Arab neighbors from the moment the nation began in 1948. They were not always at war, but they did fight many times. In the 1970s, the president of Egypt, Anwar Sadat, decided to make peace with Israel. However, the peace talks were very difficult.

When it looked like the talks would fail in 1978, President Carter decided to help. He invited Sadat and Menachem Begin, the prime minister of Israel, to come to the U.S. to talk. He took the men to Camp

| The oil shortage caused long lines at gas stations.

| President Jimmy Carter helped bring peace between Israel and Egypt.

David, a retreat for the president in Maryland. Camp David is a large, peaceful, wooded camp with comfortable cabins for the president and his guests. In this relaxed place, away from the reporters and the problems of their own nations, the two men were able to reach an agreement. It was named the Camp David Accords.

The Camp David Accords set up many parts of the peace treaty the two nations signed in 1979. That treaty ended the war between Egypt and Israel. It gave back to Egypt the Sinai Peninsula which Israel had captured. It was also Jimmy Carter's greatest success as president.

Iran and Afghanistan. Aside from the Camp David Accords, Jimmy Carter had few other successes as president. His lack of experience, which had gotten him elected, caused problems. He did not know how to work with Congress, and the American people felt like he could not lead clearly. He also faced some major problems with the rest of the world.

Jimmy Carter was a Christian man who wanted to protect the freedom of people all over the world. The problem was that many nations that were not free were also our allies against the communists. One of these was

| The Iranian hostages were freed the day Ronald Reagan became president.

Iran. Iran's ruler, the Shah, was a cruel dictator, but he was a great help to the U.S. because his nation produced oil and was so near the Soviet Union. When his people began to rebel against his rule, President Carter would not help him. The Shah left early in 1979 and a new government based on the religion of **Islam** came to power. The new government was as bad as the one under the Shah except it was not friendly to the United States.

In November of 1979, the Shah visited the United States for medical care. Angry mobs in Iran attacked the U.S. Embassy in Iran. Embassies are supposed to be protected by the local government, but the Islamic government of Iran did not protect ours. The mob took the American diplomats as hostages and demanded that the Shah be given to them in exchange. President Carter refused and the Iranian government would not release the hostages. It was unbelievable that a government would actually take another nation's diplomats as hostages! This was called the Iran Hostage Crisis.

President Carter was not able to solve the Hostage Crisis. The Iranians held the 52 American diplomats for 15 months. The president tried to negotiate, but the angry government in Iran would not listen. The president finally sent the military to try a rescue, but it failed. The strongest nation on earth could not even get its own people back. It was incredibly frustrating for the American people who followed the whole thing every day on the news.

A month after the Hostage Crisis began, the Soviet Union invaded Afghanistan, a country on their southern border. This ended Détente. The Soviet Union was trying to protect a communist government in that land. However, the Soviet army was never able to defeat the Islamic rebels who fought against them there. It was like Vietnam for the United States. The Hostage Crisis and the invasion of Afghanistan made America look very weak and helpless. People blamed Jimmy Carter for that. In 1980 they chose a new president, Republican Ronald Reagan.

Complete these sentences.

1.25   The two biggest problems in America in the 1970s were: _____
(rising prices) and the _____ (oil shortages).

1.26   In 1973 the Arab nations _____ sales of oil to the United States.

1.27   Anwar Sadat and Menachem Begin, with the help of Jimmy Carter, were able to come to an agreement in 1978 called the _____ .

1.28   In 1979 Détente ended when the Soviet Union invaded _____ .

1.29   In the _____ Crisis, 52 American diplomats were held prisoner for 15 months.

1.30   The Shah of Iran left in 1979 and a new government based on the religion of _____ took power.

1.31   OPEC stands for _____

1.32   The inflation of the 1970s was ended by the _____
_____ when it raised interest rates.

1.33   _____ was elected president in 1980.

Review the material in this section to prepare for the Self Test. The Self Test will check your understanding of this section. Any items you miss on this test will show you what areas you will need to restudy in order to prepare for the unit test.

SELF TEST 1

Match these people (each answer, 3 points).

1.01 _____ Communist ruler of China

1.02 _____ Elected president in 1980

1.03 _____ Prime minister of Israel

1.04 _____ Communist leader of the U.S.S.R.

1.05 _____ Nixon's Secretary of State

1.06 _____ Only president to resign from office

1.07 _____ President of Egypt

1.08 _____ Only appointed president

1.09 _____ Elected president because of his lack of experience

1.010 _____ Lawyer who investigated the Watergate Scandal

a. Richard Nixon

b. Jimmy Carter

c. Mao Zedong

d. Leonid Brezhnev

e. Henry Kissinger

f. Archibald Cox

g. Gerald Ford

h. Anwar Sadat

i. Menachem Begin

j. Ronald Reagan

Complete these sentences (each answer, 4 points).

1.011 The _____ Scandal forced a president to resign.

1.012 Richard Nixon was the first president to visit the communist nations of _____ and _____ .

1.013 The Cold War thaw in the 1970s was called _____ .

1.014 The two biggest problems in America in the 1970s were _____ and _____ .

1.015 Egypt and Israel were able to make peace because of the _____ _____ Accords, an agreement between their leaders made in 1978 with the help of Jimmy Carter.

1.016 The treaty to control atomic bombs was called SALT, which stands for

_____ .

1.017   Fifty-two diplomats were held hostage for 15 months by a mob in Iran during the

_____ .

1.018   The Soviet Union ended its thaw with the U.S. when it invaded the nation of

_____ on its southern border in 1979.

Answer _true_ or _false_ (each answer, 3 points).

1.019   _____   Gerald Ford made Americans very angry when he pardoned John Dean.

1.020   _____   During Détente, American presidents ended Containment.

1.021   _____   Watergate started with a burglary of the Democratic Party
headquarters.

1.022   _____   Richard Nixon recorded conversations in his office while he was president.

1.023   _____   The Federal Reserve Board was able to control inflation by raising
interest rates.

1.024   _____   Communist China has not yet taken the Chinese seat in the United
Nations.

1.025   _____   The Soviet Union needed to trade with the West to get new technology.

1.026   _____   The Soviet Union stopped "wars of liberation" during the 1970s.

1.027   _____   Many Americans began to trust the government more because of
Watergate.

1.028   _____   OPEC tried to make oil cheaper in the 1970s.

Teacher check:

Score _____

Initials _____

Date _____

80 / 100

2. REBUILDING CONFIDENCE

The 1980s were a time when America regained its confidence. Inflation was finally under control, and more jobs became available. The new president was popular, confident, and strongly anti-communist. The military, which had failed in Vietnam, succeeded in Grenada, Panama, and in 1991, the Persian Gulf. Moreover, communism began to show serious signs of changing. By the decade's end, an unexpected Cold War victory occurred that shocked and amazed the world with its speed. Thus, America, which had been so beaten and embarrassed in the 1960s and 1970s, grew confident again in the 1980s.

Objectives

Review these objectives. When you have completed this section, you should be able to:

1. Identify the presidents of this time and their actions.
3. Describe how the Cold War ended and the changes that came.
5. Describe events in America near the turn of the millennium.

Vocabulary

Study these new words. Learning the meanings of these words is a good study habit and will improve your understanding of this LIFEPAC.

attitude (at' ə tüd). A way of thinking, acting, or feeling.

invalid (in val' id). Not legally binding; not having legal force; without value.

Pronunciation Key: hat, āge, cãre, fär; let, ēqual, tėrm; it, īce; hot, ōpen, ôrder; oil; out; cup, pút, rüle; child; long; thin; /ŦH/ for then; /zh/ for measure; /u/ or /ə/ represents /a/ in about, /e/ in taken, /i/ in pencil, /o/ in lemon, and /u/ in circus.

Reagan Revolution

New attitude. Ronald Reagan's presidency began on a very happy note, the end of the Iran Hostage Crisis. Iran had gone to war with its neighbor, Iraq, in 1980. The vicious war was very expensive. Iran had money in America that Jimmy Carter was holding until the hostages were released. In exchange for the release of the hostages, the Iranians got most of their money back. However, just to be mean, they held the Americans until minutes after Ronald Reagan became president in January of 1981. Then the hostages were run through a line of chanting protesters in Iran and put on a plane for their trip home, after 444 days in captivity.

Thus, the very first thing that happened in the United States after Reagan became president was a huge party to welcome the hostages home. Many people had tied up yellow ribbons during the crisis to remember the hostages and press for their freedom. When they came home, the whole nation was decorated with yellow! The 52 men and women were taken to the White House in Washington in a huge parade through cheering crowds with yellow banners and ribbons. They were welcomed back by the president. They were given parades and parties in their towns when they went home to recover. It was a release of joy after a long, dark time.

The beginning was a good symbol of the type of president Ronald Reagan would be. He believed in America and the American way of life. He hated communism and believed his freedom-loving people could defeat it. He was very good at talking to people and getting them to listen to his ideas. He was also very popular.

| President Ronald Reagan

| President Reagan built up the military to face the threat of communism in the world.

Government changes. Reagan wanted to change the government in America. He believed that it had become too big and powerful since the Great Depression. He believed the American government should take less money from the people and do fewer things to control businesses and people. This was part of the "Reagan Revolution," because he changed the direction of the American government. Since Reagan, attempts have been made to cut government spending and controls. It was a change in **attitude** that he began.

Reagan cut taxes and spending on social programs like welfare (that paid people who were out of work). He also increased spending on the military that had begun under Jimmy Carter. However, under Reagan, the military grew more than it ever had in a time of peace. The president was determined to be ready to fight communism if necessary. The tax cuts and military spending caused huge deficits, leaving the United States deeply in debt.

Terrorism. The 1970s and 1980s were a time of *terrorism*. Terrorists try to get something done by killing and destroying. For example, the Palestine Liberation Organization (PLO) wanted a homeland for the Palestinian people in Israel. They set off bombs, kidnapped people, killed people, and hijacked travelers hoping that all their evil would force people to give them what they wanted. There were many of these terrorist groups in the 1970s and 1980s.

| Terrorists try to get what they want by killing and destroying.

Terrorists held dozens of Americans and other western people as captives in Lebanon for different reasons in the 1980s. Terrorists hijacked a TWA jet in 1985, hijacked a cruise ship that same year, and bombed a disco used by American soldiers in 1986. One of the biggest acts of terrorism was against American Marines who were in Lebanon. They were there to help with a cease fire in a civil war. Someone drove a truck loaded with explosives into their barracks in 1983, killing more than 200 men. Terrorism continues to happen today.

Foreign problems. Reagan was determined to help nations fight against communism when he was president. However, many of the fighters working against communism were very cruel themselves. One good example was in Nicaragua, in Central America.

In 1979 the country of Nicaragua was taken over by a group called the Sandinistas. They set up a communist government and started getting help from both the U.S.S.R. and Cuba. Reagan sent American aid to a group fighting them who were called the Contras. However, the Contras were cruel and, in many ways, as bad as the Sandinista. Finally, Congress forbade sending them any more money.

Reagan was frustrated by the American hostages being held in Lebanon. Many of the terrorists there were being helped by Iran. Reagan began secretly selling weapons to Iran. He hoped that would convince them to free the hostages. It did not work and it was very embarrassing when it became public. To make matters worse, some of the men who worked for the president had taken the money from the weapons sales and sent it to the Contras illegally. This scandal was called the *Iran-Contra Affair*. Several of the president's aides were arrested.

| Grenada was a pivotal point in stopping further communism in the Caribbean.

Grenada. The island of Grenada is located in the southeast Caribbean Sea just north of South America. In 1979 a communist government took over the island. The new government began to build a huge airport with Cuban help. The U.S. was afraid it would be used as a base for the Soviet Union. When a revolution broke out on the island in 1983, Reagan decided to act. He sent the U.S. army in to throw out the Cubans and set up a free government. It was a very quick, popular, and successful attack. It began to restore America's faith in our military that had been so badly damaged by Vietnam. That new faith was another part of the Reagan Revolution in America.

Answer these questions.

2.1   How do terrorists try to get what they want?

_____

_____

2.2   What was the happy event that began Ronald Reagan's presidency?

_____

2.3   What did Reagan cut spending for?_____

2.4   What did Reagan increase spending for? _____

2.5   What was the big act of terrorism against the U.S. Marines in 1983?

_____

_____

_____

2.6   Why were the 52 Iran hostages finally released? _____

_____

_____

2.7   Who were the Sandinistas and the Contras? _____

_____

_____

2.8   What was the Iran-Contra Affair? _____

_____

_____

2.9   Why did the U.S. invade Grenada in 1983 and what were the results?

_____

_____

_____

Changing Communism

China. There was a struggle in China in the 1970s between those who wanted China to be more communist and those who wanted it to be more like the West. Those who wanted it to be more like the West won the fight. Mao Zedong died in 1976 and many of his ideas died with him. Deng Xiaoping, a man who favored change, came to power. From that time on, China began to become less communist in how it worked.

China in the 1980s began to do business much like America. The large collective farms were broken apart. Families were given their own land to farm. They could plant what they wanted and keep the profits from what they sold. This change allowed China to produce much more food than it had under the communist system.

Businesses in China also began to be run by people, not the government. People who had a clever idea were allowed to use it to make money for themselves. Foreign companies were allowed to come in and set up businesses. They could sell the goods in China or ship them out to other nations. Tourists were encouraged to come and visit China's many beautiful old buildings and places. Suddenly, the Chinese people were encouraged to make money for themselves, not to serve the government, which was the normal idea in communism.

One thing in China did not change, however. The people were not allowed to have freedom. They were not allowed to say the government was wrong or try to vote for leaders who were not communists. They were not allowed to be Christians and have freedom of worship.

The many changes in China made some of the people believe they would get these freedoms. They began to protest in favor of more freedom in the late 1980s. In April of 1989, a former Chinese leader who had been in favor of more freedom died. Many

| China opened up to tourism for the first time in the 1980s.

young adults, especially students, began to march in the streets in his memory. They took over Tiananmen Square, an important plaza in the capital city of Beijing. For a while it looked like the government would allow the protests to continue; it did not, however.

The Chinese government sent in the army to drive the protesters out of Tiananmen Square. The army used tanks and rifles against the unarmed students. Hundreds were killed. After the attack, many of the leaders were arrested and sentenced to long jail terms. The Chinese people stopped protesting and were forced to keep their communist government. In the usual communist fashion, the government lied about what had happened at Tiananmen Square. It claimed a few criminals attacked the army there! The Chinese government has never admitted that its army murdered unarmed people in Tiananmen Square in 1989.

The Soviet Union. Leonid Brezhnev died in 1982. The next Soviet leader, Yuri Andropov, died in 1984. The next Soviet leader, Konstantin Chernenko died in 1985. Finally, in 1985 the Soviet Politburo (which made the important decisions) chose a man named Mikhail Gorbachev who, at 54, was a much younger man than the earlier leaders. He was also a reformer. He began to change the Soviet Union.

Gorbachev wanted the Soviet Union to become richer and more powerful. The communist system had made the Soviet Union poor for its size and potential strength. Gorbachev still wanted communism, but he realized his country was in trouble. He wanted people to work harder and better. He wanted businesses to work faster and better. He wanted them to make better goods and new technology like the Free World. He tried to change things to make this happen without getting rid of government control. It did not work. The Soviet Union could not produce high quality goods quickly. The whole communist system prevented it from happening. Since people could not get more money for faster and better work, they did not do it.

Gorbachev called his reforms *perestroika* (which means rebuilding or redoing). To get the people to support his changes he allowed them more freedom of speech. He called this *glasnost* (openness). As things in the Soviet Union got worse, the openness allowed people to know about it. The Communist Party's control over the nation began to lessen as the people were able to know what was really happening.

| Mikhail Gorbachev and President Reagan

Cold War. One of the biggest changes Gorbachev brought was to the Cold War. The cost of paying for "wars of liberation" all over the world was too much for the Soviet Union. It needed its money for problems at home. Gorbachev began to work to cut back on the fighting between the U.S. and the U.S.S.R.

President Reagan was doubtful about Gorbachev at first. He was afraid it was another communist trick—to talk peace and plan war at the same time—but President Reagan and Gorbachev met face to face three times. These meetings were called *summits*, because the men at the top (summit) of the government met. The two leaders made several important agreements that made it look like the Cold War might be ending. They signed two treaties that actually cut back on the number of atomic weapons they had. The new U.S. president elected in 1988, George H. W. Bush, continued to work with Gorbachev, and the Cold War finally did end while he was president.

Gorbachev also took the Soviet army out of Afghanistan in 1988 and 1989. He cut back the number of soldiers and weapons the Soviets kept in Europe. Thus, his actions matched his words

Mikhail Gorbachev's biggest move toward ending the Cold War was something he <u>did</u> <u>not</u> do. He made it clear that the Soviet Union would no longer use its army to force eastern Europe to stay communist. When that became clear, protests against communism began all over the Communist Bloc. That brought a year of miracles, 1989, and the end of the Cold War.

Complete these sentences.

2.10   The students who were protesting for freedom took over

_____ Square in Beijing in 1989. They were attacked by

the _____ .

2.11   The new leader of China who wanted change after Mao's death was

_____ .

2.12   _____ Soviet leaders died between 1980 and 1986.

2.13   The leader who changed the Soviet Union and ended the Cold War was

_____ .

2.14   The reforms of Mikhail Gorbachev were called _____

(rebuilding) and _____ (openness).

2.15   The Soviet army left _____ in 1988 and 1989.

2.16   Reagan and Gorbachev signed treaties that _____ the

number of nuclear weapons their countries had.

2.17   A meeting between the leaders of two nations is called a _____ .

Answer these questions.

2.18   How did businesses and farms change in China in the 1980s?

_____

_____

_____

HISTORY & GEOGRAPHY 509

LIFEPAC TEST

NAME _____

DATE _____

SCORE _____

Answer *true* or *false*. If the answer is false, change one or more of the underlined words to make it true (3 points each). (Take off 1 point if the student answers false correctly, but gives the wrong correction).

1. _____ The U.S. led a coalition to drive Iraq out of Kuwait in the <u>Desert</u> War.

2. _____ Fifty-two American diplomats were held as prisoners for 444 days in the <u>Iran-Contra Affair</u>.

3. _____ The U.S. invaded Grenada and <u>Panama</u> in the 1980s.

4. _____ China and <u>Hungary</u> were still communist after the Cold War.

5. _____ Two of the biggest problems in America in the 1970s were the energy crisis and <u>deficits</u>.

6. _____ The U.S. sent soldiers into <u>Somalia</u> in 1992 so that food could be delivered to starving people there.

7. _____ <u>SALT</u>, which was negotiated in the U.S. with the help of President Jimmy Carter, was the basis for peace between Israel and Egypt.

8. _____ The <u>Soviet Union</u> broke apart after some old communist leaders tried and failed to re-establish communism there.

9. _____ Détente ended when the Soviet Union invaded <u>Poland</u> in 1979.

10. _____ Students who protested in Tiananmen Square in the capital of <u>Yugoslavia</u> were attacked by the army.

Complete these sentences (each answer, 3 points).

11. In the 1970s and 1980s, communism in _____ changed as the government gave businesses and farms back to the people and encouraged them to make money.

12. *Perestroika* and *glasnost* were reforms in the communist nation of _____ _____ .

13. The Cold War and communism in Europe ended in the year _____ .

14. Jean-Bernard Aristide, the president of _____ , was overthrown by the army in 1991.

15. The former communist nation of _____ has been torn apart by fighting between Serbs, Croats, Muslims, and Albanians.

16. In the _____ Scandal, aides close to the president hired burglars to break into the Democratic Party headquarters.

17. _____ was an organization of countries that exported oil that drove gas prices up in the 1970s.

18. The _____ Scandal forced a president to resign before he could be impeached.

19. In 1983 terrorists blew up a Marine barracks in the country of _____ , killing more than 200 Americans.

20. Gerald Ford angered the American public when he gave a _____ to Richard Nixon.

21. The region of _____ in the African nation of the Sudan has suffered war, famine, and disease.

22. The U.S. invaded _____ in an effort to find Osama bin Laden.

23. The worst tsunami ever recorded occurred in the _____ .

Choose the president associated with each item. Some answers will be used more than once (each answer, 2 points).

24. _____ Created a revolution in thinking about government; fought communism

25. _____ Elected because he had no experience in Washington and people were sick of the old government

26. _____ Invasion of Haiti

27. _____ Second president to go through the impeachment process

28. _____ First president to visit China and the U.S.S.R.

29. _____ Formed the coalition against Iraq

30. _____ Iran-Contra Affair

31. _____ President during the September 11, 2001 terrorist attacks

32. _____ First appointed president

33. _____ Savings and Loan Crisis

34. _____ Could not solve the Iran Hostage Crisis

a. George H. W. Bush
b. Bill Clinton
c. Richard Nixon
d. Gerald Ford
e. Jimmy Carter
f. Ronald Reagan
g. George W. Bush

Match these people (each answer, 2 points).

35.	_____ President of Egypt	a.	Saddam Hussein
36.	_____ Leader of the terrorist group Al Qaeda	b.	Osama Bin Laden
37.	_____ Leader of China	c.	Boris Yeltsin
38.	_____ Drug smuggler, military leader in Panama	d.	Jean-Bernard Aristide
		e.	Anwar Sadat
39.	_____ President of Russia	f.	Mikhail Gorbachev
40.	_____ Prime Minister of Israel	g.	Henry Kissinger
41.	_____ American Secretary of State	h.	Menachem Begin
42.	_____ President of Haiti	i.	Deng Xiaoping
43.	_____ Last president of the U.S.S.R.	j.	Manuel Noriega
44.	_____ Dictator of Iraq		

2.19   What did Gorbachev say he would not do in eastern Europe?

_____

_____

_____

2.20   Why did Gorbachev want to change things in the Soviet Union?

_____

_____

_____

2.21   Why did Gorbachev want to stop fighting the Cold War?

_____

_____

_____

Miracle Year

Annus mirabilis. The year 1989 was called _annus mirabilis_, the miracle year. Communism had controlled Eastern Europe since 1945. The people had not known freedom for almost fifty years, but freedom surprised everyone by coming in 1989. Many of the governments in east Europe changed that year because the Soviet Union's army was no longer threatening to invade. In Poland, the leaders of Solidarity, the free union of the early 1980s, signed an agreement with the communist government in 1989. It allowed the country to have its first free elections since World War II. When Czechoslovakia had the chance for reform in 1989, there were huge protests in the streets in favor of democracy and freedom. The communist government resigned in November because of the protests. A new, non-communist government was formed. The nations of Bulgaria and Romania soon followed in ending the communist rule of their governments.

The most dramatic events of 1989 occurred in Germany. The people of East Germany began to protest for freedom in 1989. However, they also began to leave. They could go to Hungary which had opened its border with the West in 1989. From there, the East German people would go to West Germany and become free citizens of that country. Thousands began to leave. Whole train loads, especially of young people, rode out of East Germany to Hungary to Austria to West Germany. Communist East Germany was losing large numbers of people every day. Realizing they had no choice, the eastern government announced on November 9, 1989 that the border with West Germany was open. East Germans could cross any time they wanted. That night thousands of people in Berlin began to climb over the Berlin Wall to greet their fellow Berliners on the other side. They began to use hammers, rocks, cranes, and bulldozers to tear down the Wall. Within a few months, the most important symbol of the Cold War was gone and Berlin was one city again. Germany was reunited as one nation with a democratic government the very next year. Soon all of the former communist nations of Eastern Europe had free elections. Historians say that the Cold War ended in 1989.

| Foundation of the Berlin Wall; a plaque in the ground commemorates the end of communism in 1989.

Other events. The remarkable events in Europe did not stop more ordinary problems in America. In 1989 President George H. W. Bush signed a law to end the Savings and Loan Crisis. This crisis happened because many banks (called savings and loans) were in trouble in the 1980s. They had made bad loans, the people who worked there had stolen their money, and easy rules had caused waste. Some of these banks had to close because they did not have enough money to pay people who had accounts with them. These businesses were insured by the federal

| The U.S. invaded Panama to protect the canal and arrest Noriega for drug smuggling.

government under laws passed after the Great Depression. The government took over the troubled banks, sold some, closed others, and paid off their debts. It cost the U.S. government hundreds of billions of dollars.

The U.S. Army also continued to recover its respect in 1989 when America invaded Panama. The army of Panama was led by a corrupt man named Manuel Noriega in the 1980s. He was making money by smuggling drugs. A U.S. court accused him of it in 1988. The president of Panama tried to fire him because of that, but Noriega's friends forced the president to resign instead. In 1989 Panama held new elections and a man who opposed Noriega won. However, Noriega declared the elections **invalid** and would not allow the new president to take office.

The U.S. had a treaty with Panama which was slowly giving the country control of the Panama Canal, but it also allowed the U.S. Army to protect it. When a U.S. soldier stationed in Panama was killed in December of 1989, President George H. W. Bush ordered the army to overthrow Noriega. The invasion went quickly and easily. Noriega eventually surrendered, was tried in the

U.S., and was put in jail for drug smuggling. The man who won the elections in 1989 became president of Panama. The quick success again added to the growing trust between the American people, the military, and the government.

Name the person, place, event, or thing.

2.22 _____ Crisis that cost the U.S. government billions of dollars in the 1980s

2.23 _____ Year the Cold War ended

2.24 _____ Free union in Poland, won all the elected offices in 1989

2.25 _____ Country invaded by the U.S. in 1989

2.26 _____ Military leader of Panama, convicted of smuggling drugs

2.27 _____ U.S. president when the Cold War ended

Answer these questions.

2.28 Why was 1989 called the miracle year?

_____

_____

2.29 Why did East Germany open its border?

_____

_____

Review the material in this section to prepare for the Self Test. The Self Test will check your understanding of this section and the previous section. Any items you miss on this test will show you what areas you will need to restudy in order to prepare for the unit test.

SELF TEST 2

Answer these questions (points for each answer are after the question).

2.01   Why was 1989 a miracle year? Give at least two examples. (10 points)

_____

_____

_____

_____

_____

2.02   What was the Watergate Scandal and how did it end? (5 points)

_____

_____

_____

_____

_____

2.03   How did communism change in China in the 1970s and '80s? (5 points)

_____

_____

_____

_____

Complete these sentences (each answer, 3 points).

2.04   The Iran Hostage Crisis ended on the day _____

became president.

2.05   Iran ended the Hostage Crisis because it needed money for a _____ with Iraq .

2.06   The Sandinista government was fighting the American-supported Contras in the

nation of _____ .

2.07   Under Ronald Reagan, the U.S. invaded the island nation of _____

to stop communism there.

2.08   The students who protested in Tiananmen Square in Beijing were attacked by

_____ .

2.09   The reform in the U.S.S.R. called *glasnost* meant _____ .

2.010   The Soviet army withdrew from _____ in 1988 and 1989.

2.011   The failure of many banks called the _____

Crisis cost the U.S. government billions of dollars in the 1980s.

2.012   Under President George H. W. Bush, the U.S. Army invaded _____

to overthrow the military leader there.

2.013   A meeting between the leaders of two nations is called a _____ .

Match these people (each answer, 2 points).

2.014 _____ Military leader of Panama, jailed in the U.S. for drug smuggling

2.015 _____ U.S. president, changed the attitude of the government toward less control and taxes

2.016 _____ Leader of China, wanted to make it more like the West

2.017 _____ Leader of China who wanted real communism

2.018 _____ Prime Minister of Israel

2.019 _____ U.S. president when the Cold War ended

2.020 _____ U.S. president during the Iran Hostage Crisis

2.021 _____ President of Egypt

2.022 _____ First U.S. president to visit communist China and the U.S.S.R.

2.023 _____ Secretary of State for President Nixon

2.024 _____ Only appointed president in U.S. history

2.025 _____ Leader of the Soviet Union, his reforms caused the end of the Cold War

a. Mikhail Gorbachev

b. Ronald Reagan

c. Mao Zedong

d. Richard Nixon

e. Jimmy Carter

f. Henry Kissinger

g. George H. W. Bush

h. Deng Xiaoping

i. Manuel Noriega

j. Gerald Ford

k. Anwar Sadat

l. Menachem Begin

Answer *true* or *false* (each answer, 2 points).

2.026 _____ Terrorists kill and kidnap to try to get something they want done.

2.027 _____ The Iran-Contra Affair was a scandal under President George H. W. Bush about the Contras kidnapping Iranian officials.

2.028 _____ Inflation was one of the biggest problems in America in the 1970s.

2.029 _____ Reagan and Gorbachev signed the first treaty between the U.S. and U.S.S.R. that cut back the number of atomic bombs each side had.

2.030 _____ The Camp David Accords were the basis for a treaty between the U.S. and Israel.

2.031 _____ The Energy Crisis was a time in the 1970s when there was a shortage of oil causing prices to rise quickly.

2.032 _____ The Soviet Union needed reform and trade with the West because it could not produce high-quality goods and new technology.

2.033 _____ America regained some confidence in its government and military in the 1980s.

2.034 _____ SALT was a treaty to increase trade between the U.S. and China.

2.035 _____ Gerald Ford pardoned Richard Nixon.

2.036 _____ OPEC is an organization of nations that export oil.

2.037 _____ Terrorists blew up a U.S. Marine barracks in Lebanon in 1983.

2.038 _____ *Perestroika* was very successful in improving manufacturing in the communist Soviet Union.

	Teacher check:	Initials _____	80
✓	Score _____	Date _____	100

3. AFTER THE COLD WAR

The end of the Cold War brought many changes to the U.S. and the world. The world was no longer divided into two large groups fighting for control of the world. Communism was no longer a threat. America was the only superpower. These changes made many things better and unfortunately some things worse.

Problems in the Persian Gulf region soon showed America that the loss of communism did not necessarily make the world a safer place. America would need to address the problems of dictators and terrorists as it entered the New Millennium. The nation would find that it needed to protect its citizens at home and around the world.

Objectives

Review these objectives. When you have completed this section, you should be able to:

1. Identify the presidents of this time and their actions.
3. Describe how the Cold War ended and the changes that came.
4. Describe the first Persian Gulf War and the events surrounding it.
5. Describe events in America shortly before and after the New Millennium.

Vocabulary

Study these new words. Learning the meanings of these words is a good study habit and will improve your understanding of this LIFEPAC.

accurate (ak' yər it). Exactly right; correct.

clan (klan). A group of related families that claim to be descended from a common ancestor.

coalition (kō ə lish' ən). A temporary alliance of different parties, persons, or nations for joint action.

dismantle (dis man' tl). To pull down; take apart.

oath (ōth). A statement that something is true or a solemn promise, which God or some holy person or thing is called to witness.

plot (plot). A secret plan, especially to do something wrong.

tsunami (sū nä' mē). A great sea wave produced especially by submarine earth movement or volcanic eruption.

Pronunciation Key: hat, āge, cãre, fär; let, ēqual, tėrm; it, īce; hot, ōpen, ôrder; oil; out; cup, put, rüle; child; long; thin; /ŦH/ for then; /zh/ for measure; /u/ or /ə/ represents /a/ in about, /e/ in taken, /i/ in pencil, /o/ in lemon, and /u/ in circus.

The First Persian Gulf War

Iraq. In 1990 the dictator of Iraq was a brutal man named Saddam Hussein. He had fought a war with Iran which began in 1980 and ended in 1988. The war left Iraq deeply in debt. One of the nations Hussein owed money to was the oil-rich nation of Kuwait, south of Iraq. Iraq and Kuwait disagreed over the location of their border and who could pump oil from underground oil sources that were beneath both countries. Hussein also claimed that Kuwait was really a part of Iraq. Hussein used all these things as excuses to invade Kuwait in August of 1990 to take over their oil wealth.

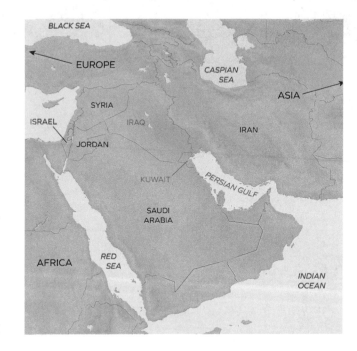

The Iraqi army was the fifth largest in the world. Kuwait only had a small army. Within one day, Kuwait was occupied by Iraq. Saddam Hussein claimed it was now part of Iraq. His soldiers began to steal and destroy many of the valuable things the wealthy Kuwaiti people had in their homes and stores. The ruler of Kuwait, the Emir, and many of his people fled to Saudi Arabia.

American reaction. After Saddam Hussein invaded Kuwait, he moved his army to the border of Saudi Arabia. It looked like he might try to invade that nation as well. Both Saudi Arabia and Kuwait were friendly with the United States. Those two nations supplied much of the oil needed by the industrial nations of the West. They did not want Hussein to have the power that so much oil wealth could give him. President George H. W. Bush built a coalition of almost forty nations to stop Iraq, working closely with the United Nations. Many of the coalition members were Arab nations that were willing to fight with the U.S. to stop Iraq from taking over Kuwait. The U.N. told the coalition to use force to free Kuwait if Iraq did not leave by January 15, 1991.

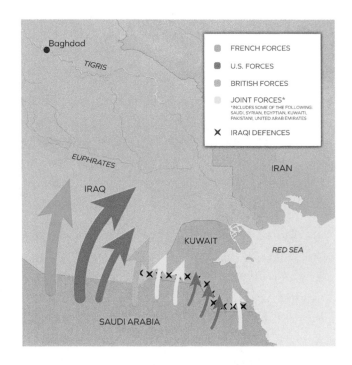

The Persian Gulf War began on January 17, 1991 with five weeks of intense bombing that was code-named Operation Desert Storm. The Iraqi capital, Baghdad, was bombed every day. Saddam Hussein refused to surrender. When the coalition began a ground war on February 24, 1991, the Iraqi soldiers did not want to fight the coalition. The heavy bombing had destroyed what little will they had to fight. The Desert Sabre ground offensive retook Kuwait in about 100 hours of ground fighting. President Bush ordered the war stopped after Kuwait was retaken. Hussein accepted terms of a formal cease fire in April.

The Persian Gulf War was an incredible victory for the U.N. and the United States. The people of Kuwait staged huge celebrations as the coalition members freed their nation. The people of Iraq rebelled against Saddam Hussein, but he was able to crush the revolt and stay in power.

Name the person, place, event, or thing.

3.1 _____ Dictator of Iraq

3.2 _____ Nation invaded by Iraq in the Persian Gulf War

3.3 _____ President who put together the Persian Gulf War coalition

3.4 _____ Number of hours of ground war

3.5 _____ Organization that condemned Iraq's invasion and told the coalition to use force to drive them out

3.6 _____ Many were afraid Iraq would invade this nation after Kuwait

More Changes

The fall of the U.S.S.R. In 1991 the Soviet Union fell apart. If that had not happened, the Cold War might have started again. The Soviet Union was a huge country made up many nations, called republics, joined into one. These people and nations had been forced to join the U.S.S.R. The republics, like the states in America, had their own governments. The Soviet Union reduced the power of the Communist Party, having fairly free elections in 1989 and even freer ones in 1990. Mikhail Gorbachev, however, never faced a real election. The newly elected representatives felt they must support the people, not Gorbachev.

The republics of the Soviet Union began to work for more independence. Among the new leaders working this way was Boris Yeltsin, the elected president of the Republic of Russia. Many of the old leaders of the Communist Party were furious at the reforms and changes. They did not like the fact that the Soviet republics were becoming more independent. The old communist leaders tried to take over the government of the Soviet Union in August of 1991 and put communism back in power. They arrested Mikhail Gorbachev and held him prisoner at his vacation home. The communist leaders had not counted on Boris Yeltsin, however. Yeltsin spoke to the people of Russia and asked them to fight against the communists. The people came to the government buildings where he was, surrounded them, and protected their elected leaders. The leaders of the **plot** ordered the army to remove them and arrest Yeltsin,

| The former Soviet Union

but many of the officers refused to obey. The plot failed and the communist leaders were arrested. The fact that Yeltsin had stopped the communist leaders made him the most powerful man in the Soviet Union.

He and the other national leaders decided to **dismantle** the Soviet Union. Each of the republics voted for independence before the year had passed. On December 25, 1991, Mikhail Gorbachev resigned as the president of the Soviet Union and it ceased to exist. The Cold War was really finished.

| President George H. W. Bush and Boris Yeltsin

Problems. The collapse of the Soviet Union caused some new problems. The U.S.S.R. had a huge collection of atomic bombs. The U.S. did not want these to fall into the hands of terrorists or nations that would not be careful with them. Several wars broke out in the new nations. The U.S. signed several treaties to control the atomic weapons, sent some help for businesses, and tried to help negotiate for peace in the wars.

Democracy. With the collapse of the Soviet Union, the only communist governments left were in Cuba, Vietnam, North Korea, and China. All over the world, democracy began to appear in nations where it had repeatedly failed. This was because the Cold War was over. During the Cold War, dictators could get aid from one or the other super powers to keep themselves in power. Now that aid was gone. Many countries in the Third World were forced to hold elections because the dictators no longer could get money and support for their own power. However, many were not able to stay democratic as civil wars and military governments ended the new governments.

| The collapse of the U.S.S.R. dried up money for several small dictators around the world.

Deficits. In America in the early 1990s, the huge deficits became a major issue. Republican President George H. W. Bush and the Democratic Congress were not able to control them. In 1990 a recession began (a small depression), putting people out of work and closing businesses. The deficit was so big that it was impossible for the government to spend money to pull the country out of it. Bush had been unbelievably popular after the Persian Gulf War. However, as the recession and the deficits continued, he became unpopular, especially after he broke a firm promise not to raise taxes. He lost the 1992 election to Bill Clinton, the governor of Arkansas.

Somalia. The nation of Somalia, on the east coast of Africa, was in serious trouble in 1992. Clans within the country, led by warlords, were fighting each other for control of the land. Crops had been destroyed and people were dying of hunger. The United Nations and other charities tried to bring in food. However, the clans would steal it or demand money to allow it to be delivered. Thousands of people were dying because the food could not get to them. In December of 1992, just before he left office, George H. W. Bush ordered the U.S. military to lead a U.N. force into Somalia to restore order and allow food to be delivered. Soon food began to reach the starving people. The new president Bill Clinton decided

| Somalia warlord Mohamed Aidid stole the food and starved the people, and the U.S. had to send troops to help the people.

to use the forces there to restore the government. An attempt was made to capture one of the uncooperative warlords in October of 1993. Seventy-five Americans were wounded in the attempt, and the warlord escaped. The U.N. forces were withdrawn without setting up a new government.

| A convoy of United Nations peacekeeping units

Answer *true* or *false*.

3.7 _____ Boris Yeltsin was the elected leader of the Russian Republic.

3.8 _____ The old communist regime tried to take over the government of the Soviet Union in August, 1991.

3.9 _____ Mikhail Gorbachev was the freely elected president of the Soviet Union.

3.10 _____ George H. W. Bush won the election in 1992 because he was so popular after the Persian Gulf War.

3.11 _____ The U.S. invaded Somalia in 1992 to overthrow the government there.

3.12 _____ America went into a recession in 1990.

3.13 _____ People were dying of hunger in Somalia because the clans fighting each other would not let food be delivered safely.

3.14 _____ Deficits were a problem for America in the early 1900s.

3.15 _____ Boris Yeltsin led the group that tried to overthrow Gorbachev in 1991.

3.16 _____ One of the problems after the Soviet Union broke apart was what was going to happen to all of its atomic weapons.

3.17 _____ The U.N. was able to set up a new government in Somalia.

3.18 _____ Mikhail Gorbachev resigned as president of the Soviet Union in December, 1991.

3.19 _____ Boris Yeltsin was the main reason the plot by the old communist leaders failed.

3.20 _____ In the early 1990s, free elections were held in many Third World countries because of the end of the Cold War.

3.21 _____ Cuba and China were the only communist nations after 1991.

America before the New Millennium

Yugoslavia. Yugoslavia was another communist nation made up of many people divided into republics. The Serb, Croat, Muslim, and Albanian people in Yugoslavia distrusted each other. They had cooperated under communism because the government forced them to, but they began fighting as soon as they were free to do so. Yugoslavia held free elections in 1990, and in 1991 the republics began to declare themselves independent. The Serbs and Croats in the Republic of Croatia began fighting each other in a civil war in 1991 for control of that land. The same thing happened in Bosnia when it voted for independence in 1992. The Croats and Muslims fought with the Serbs who did not want independence. In both cases, Serbia helped the Serb people fight the brutal wars. Serbia also attacked Kosovo, one of its own provinces which has mostly Albanian people in 1998 and 1999.

| The divided Yugoslavia

The United States was not willing to get deeply involved in these wars. The people of this region had been fighting each other for generations. (It was where World War I began.) The U.S. was afraid of trying to stop civil wars and having no way to end them. Even when there was proof that the Serbs were massacring people and forcing towns full of people to leave, the U.S. did not send in its army. Instead, the U.S. used negotiations, embargoes, and air attacks to push for peace, with some success. The U.S. also helped to supply soldiers as part of the U.N. forces sent there to keep the peace after an agreement, but the region continued to be unsettled and dangerous.

NAFTA. Since World War II, the nations of Europe have been working to form a union that is like a United States of Europe. It is called the European Union. The member nations were able to increase trade among themselves by ending all trade restrictions and tariffs. The U.S. watched this success and decided to copy it. President George H. W. Bush wanted such a free trade zone in North America. A treaty to allow free trade with Canada was signed in 1988. This treaty, called NAFTA (the North American Free Trade Agreement) was expanded to include Mexico in 1992. NAFTA gradually ended all trade restrictions and tariffs on all goods between the U.S., Canada, and Mexico. The Senate approved it in 1993 and it went into effect on January 1, 1994.

Deficits. America came out of the recession in 1992 and began a time of prosperity. This brought more income for the government which helped cut the deficits. Also, the Democratic Congress and President Clinton began to cut spending to decrease the deficits. In 1994 the

Republicans took control of Congress for the first time in 40 years. They cut spending even more, so the deficits continued to grow smaller and smaller in the late 1990s.

Caribbean problems. Since the 1960s The U.S.S.R. had sent Cuba a tremendous amount of money to keep its communist government working. Without that money, Cuba quickly fell into poverty. Castro, Cuba's leader would not give up communism. He did, however, begin allowing people to leave. So many left, that President Clinton began to refuse to allow them into the United States in 1994. America had always allowed Cubans trying to escape communism into the U.S. before that time.

Refugees were also coming to the United States from Haiti. The elected president in that country had been overthrown by the army in 1991. The U.S. tried, without success, to pressure the military government to restore President Jean-Bertrand Aristide. Finally, in 1994 President Clinton threatened to use the U.S. Army to put Aristide back in power. Former President Jimmy Carter (who had acted as a diplomat for many problems since being president) convinced the military government to resign just hours before the U.S. invasion was to begin. The American soldiers landed peacefully and helped the Haitian president restart his government.

Impeachment. President Clinton became involved in a scandal in 1998. He committed some immoral acts after he became president. Stories about it became public and he lied about his involvement. Because he lied about it under **oath**, he was required to give evidence in a court case. The truth came out in August of 1998. However, he would not admit he had lied in the court case. The House of Representatives, which was still controlled by the Republicans, voted to impeach the president on two charges of perjury (lying under oath) and obstruction of justice (trying to stop the court from finding out the truth). Early in 1999, a trial was held in the Senate according to the rules in the Constitution. It was only the second impeachment trial for a president in U.S. history. He was acquitted, meaning he was not removed from office.

| President Bill Clinton

Complete these sentences.

3.22 _____ was a communist nation of many

republics and people, like Croats, Serbs, and Muslims.

3.23 The U.S., Canada, and Mexico agreed to create a free trade zone under

_____ .

3.24 The United States did not want to get involved in the wars in the former Yugoslavian

republics of _____ and _____ ,

or when Serbs attacked Albanians in their own province of _____ .

3.25 Due to cuts in spending and prosperity, the _____ grew

smaller in the late 1990s.

3.26 In 1994 President Clinton stopped allowing refugees from _____

to come into the U.S. freely.

3.27 The U.S. threatened to use force to restore Jean-Bernard Aristide, the president of

_____ .

3.28 _____ was the second U.S. president impeached.

3.29 The island of _____ stayed communist and became very poor after

the Soviet Union stopped giving it money.

3.30 Former president _____ convinced the military government in

Haiti to give up power.

3.31 NAFTA was based on the success of the free trade in Europe under the

_____ .

3.32 Bill Clinton _____ under oath in a court case about his immoral actions.

America after the New Millennium

War on terrorism. In 2001 George W. Bush became the 43rd president of the United States. President Bush had been in office less than a year when terrorists attacked the U.S. on September 11, 2001. Terrorists hijacked four planes that morning. Two were flown into the twin towers of the World Trade Center in New York City. All those aboard the planes were killed and even more when the buildings burned and collapsed. Another plane was flown into the Pentagon in Washington D.C. Again all of those on board along with others in the building died. Finally a fourth hijacked plane crashed in the Pennsylvania countryside after passengers attempted to retake the plane before it could be used as a weapon. By the end of the day, over 3,000 people had died as a result of the attacks.

The U.S. Capitol, the White House, and other federal buildings in Washington D.C. were evacuated. The president and other key leaders were moved to safe locations. All air traffic in the U.S. was shut down. Investigations into the attacks soon revealed that a terrorist named Osama bin Laden was behind the plan.

Osama bin Laden headed an organization known as Al Qaeda. The organization was first headquartered in the Sudan and later moved to Afghanistan. The group targeted the U.S. in part because of its influence and military presence in the Persian Gulf region. Following the September 11 attacks, the United States worked to capture bin Laden and his associates. The United States began fighting in Afghanistan in an effort to capture bin

| President George W. Bush

| The September 11 attacks killed more Americans than Pearl Harbor.

| An F-16 pilot looks down on the Pentagon.

Laden and remove the government who was supporting him. Afghanistan soon fell and turned to a democratic form of government. Osama bin Laden was not captured and was believed to be hiding in a remote mountainous region. He was later killed by Navy SEALS during a raid on his compound in Abbottabad, Pakistan on May 2, 2011.

The United States also targeted Saddam Hussein in Iraq. For years Saddam Hussein had terrorized his own people. He was also accused of harboring terrorists. George W. Bush ordered a military invasion of Iraq in 2003. By the end of the year, the former dictator had been captured. He was later tried by the Iraqi people and sentenced to death. The U.S. had freed the Iraqi people from their dictator, but violence continued to erupt across the country. The United States army kept a force in Iraq until the end of 2011 to help the newly elected leaders and their people.

Darfur. The Darfur region in the eastern African nation of Sudan has received attention in the United States and around the world. The Sudan, the largest African nation, is about one quarter of the size of the United States. The nation has experienced frequent wars, drought, and famine. Overpopulation and once fertile land turning to desert has created many problems for the nation as well as conflicts among the different ethnic and religious groups.

| Civil war in Darfur has kept aid from reaching the refugee camps.

The tragic results of these many wars and famines can be seen in the area of Darfur. Since 2003 between 200,000 and 400,000 people living in Darfur have died as a result of the conflict. Over 1.5 million people have been forced out of their homes. The majority of these people now live in refugee camps where there is not adequate food, water, or medicine. Diseases quickly spread causing even more death and hardship for the people of Darfur.

Religious and social groups in the United States and around the world have worked to raise awareness about what has been happening in Darfur. Many agencies in the United States have sent food and other resources to help the refugees. Unfortunately, not all of these supplies reach the people they are intended to help. Both Presidents George W. Bush and Barack Obama have met with people from organizations who want to help the people of Darfur. The U.S. government continues to work to find ways to find a solution to the problems in the western Sudan. Reports available near the end of 2016 estimated that over two million people where still displaced by the conflict. Some online research could be done to see if the situation has changed since then.

Environment. Issues involving the environment are important both to Americans and people around the world. Candidates for president and other offices frequently discuss the environment in their campaigns. The United States works alone and with other nations to find ways to better care for the environment.

In 1997 meetings were held in Kyoto, Japan to try to find ways to lower the amount of greenhouse gases released into the environment. The plan agreed upon became known as the Kyoto Protocol. The plan asked that industrialized nations cut their emission levels by 2012 to 5% less than they were in 1990. Over 55 nations signed the agreement. The United States did not.

| A carbon dioxide layer traps harmful radiation and gases by bouncing them back to Earth rather than letting them escape into space.

Over 35% of the world's greenhouse gas emissions come from the United States. President George W. Bush said that signing the agreement would damage the U.S. economy. Other American leaders questioned the agreement's findings about climate change. Still others thought that the agreement did not go far enough asking for climate changes. The Kyoto Protocols did make Americans and others recognize the need to work together to take better care of the environment.

Indian Ocean tsunami. The worst tsunami ever recorded in history occurred on December 26, 2004. A tsunami is a large ocean wave (or a series of waves) caused by an underwater earthquake or a volcanic eruption. On that day, an earthquake occurred under the ocean off the west coast of the Indonesian island of Sumatra. Soon the killer waves traveled toward land. Eleven countries along the coastline of the Indian Ocean were impacted.

More than 150,000 people were dead or missing after the Indian Ocean tsunami. About a third of these were children. Millions of people were homeless. There were shortages of food, water, and medicine. People feared the spread of cholera, typhoid, and other disease. Nations from around the world worked to provide assistance. Former Presidents George H. W. Bush and Bill Clinton worked together to raise awareness about the needs of the tsunami victims.

The United States gave millions of dollars in aid to the tsunami victims. The U.S. military sent the hospital ship *Mercy* to the region. Victims of the tsunami could be treated on board the ship. The military also sent in helicopters with food and other supplies to help relieve the suffering of the people.

Finish each sentence.

3.33   On September 11, 2001, terrorists hijacked _____ U. S. airplanes.

3.34   The United States did not join other nations in signing the _____ protocol.

3.35   Al Qaeda trained in the Sudan before moving to _____ .

3.36   The U.S. sent the military hospital ship _____ to help the tsunami victims.

3.37   The terrorist who planned the September 11, 2001 attacks was named

_____ .

3.38   The worst tsunami ever recorded was in the _____ Ocean.

3.39   The largest African nation is _____ .

3.40   Former Presidents George H. W. Bush and _____

worked together to help raise funds for tsunami victims.

3.41   _____ is a region in Africa that has experienced frequent wars and famine.

3.42   The U.S. Army removed the dictator Saddam Hussein from power in _____ .

Before you take this last Self Test, you may want to do one or more of these self checks.

1.   _____   Read the objectives. See if you can do them.

2.   _____   Restudy the material related to any objectives that you cannot do.

3.   _____   Use the **SQ3R** study procedure to review the material:

     a.   **S**can the sections.

     b.   **Q**uestion yourself.

     c.   **R**ead to answer your questions.

     d.   **R**ecite the answers to yourself.

     e.   **R**eview areas you did not understand.

4.   _____   Review all vocabulary, activities, and Self Tests, writing a correct answer for every wrong answer.

SELF TEST 3

Match these people (each answer, 2 points).

3.01 _____ Leader of China, wanted it to be like the West

3.02 _____ U.S. president, distrusted communists, invaded Grenada, Iran-Contra Affair

3.03 _____ President of Haiti

3.04 _____ Dictator of Iraq

3.05 _____ U.S. president who formed the coalition against Iraq

3.06 _____ Last president of the Soviet Union

3.07 _____ Elected president of the Republic of Russia

3.08 _____ Only U.S. president to resign from office

3.09 _____ Second U.S. president to go through the impeachment process

a. Saddam Hussein
b. George H. W. Bush
c. Bill Clinton
d. Richard Nixon
e. Boris Yeltsin
f. Mikhail Gorbachev
g. Jean-Bernard Aristide
h. Deng Xiaoping
i. Ronald Reagan

Name the person, place, thing, or event (each answer, 3 points).

3.010 _____ War to free Kuwait from Iraq

3.011 _____ These were huge early in the 1990s, but grew smaller due to cuts in spending and prosperity

3.012 _____ Created a free trade zone between the U.S., Canada, and Mexico

3.013 _____ Former communist country that had several wars between Serbs, Croats, Muslims, and Albanians

3.014 _____ One of the four nations still communist after the fall of the Soviet Union

3.015 _____ Crisis in which diplomats in Iran were held prisoner for 444 days

3.016 _____ Scandal in the 1970s that forced a president to resign

3.017 _____ President of the U.S. during the September 11, 2001 terrorist attacks

3.018 _____ He planned the terrorist attacks against the U.S. in 2001

3.019 _____ The worst tsunami ever recorded occurred here

3.020 _____ The meetings regarding the Kyoto Protocol were held in this nation.

3.021 _____ Darfur is a region in this African nation

Answer these questions (each answer, 4 points).

3.022 Why did Iraq invade Kuwait?

_____

_____

_____

3.023 What did the old communist leaders do that destroyed the Soviet Union in 1991?

_____

_____

_____

3.024 Why did so many Third World countries have free elections in the 1990s?

_____

_____

_____

3.025 Why did the U.S. send soldiers into Somalia in 1992?

_____

_____

_____

3.026   What happened to the Soviet Union when it broke apart?

_____

3.027   What was the Savings and Loan Crisis of the 1980s?

_____

_____

_____

3.028   Why was 1989 a miracle year?

_____

_____

3.029   What was SALT?

_____

_____

3.030   How did communism change in China in the 1970s and 1980s?

_____

_____

Answer _true_ or _false_ (each answer, 2 points).

3.031   _____   The U.S. coalition attacked Kuwait and Iraq only directly along the
Kuwaiti border.

3.032   _____   The war against Iraq in the first Gulf War led to a great deal of prestige
for the U.S.

3.033   _____   Colin Powell was the military leader of Panama.

3.034   _____   The Soviet Union destroyed all of its atomic weapons before it dissolved.

3.035   _____   The United Nations was not able to set up a government in Somalia.

3.036   _____   The problems in Darfur have only been caused by civil war.

3.037   _____   The United States joined other nations in signing the Kyoto Protocol.

3.038   _____   Saddam Hussein was tried by the Iraqi people for his crimes.

3.039 _____ The September 11 terrorists hijacked four airplanes.

3.040 _____ The Kyoto Protocol was an agreement to lower greenhouse gas emissions.

✔	**Teacher check:**	Initials _____	**88**
	Score _____	Date _____	**110**

Before you take the LIFEPAC Test, you may want to do one or more of these self checks.

1. _____ Read the objectives. See if you can do them.
2. _____ Restudy the material related to any objectives that you cannot do.
3. _____ Use the **SQ3R** study procedure to review the material.
4. _____ Review activities, Self Tests, and LIFEPAC vocabulary words.
5. _____ Restudy areas of weakness indicated by the last Self Test.

NOTES